How to Avoid Foreclosure in California, 2012 Edition

An Easy Guide to Saving Your Property or Walking Away With Cash

Howard L. Hibbard, Attorney

Published by Cheka Press
Burlingame, California

Published by Cheka Press
251 Park Road, Suite 800
Burlingame, CA 94010-4232

Book designed and edited by Brenda Krauss.

For legal services regarding complex real property matters from construction defect to foreclosures, or business litigation from corporate issues to bankruptcy adversary actions, please contact:

Law Office of Howard L. Hibbard
251 Park Road, Suite 800
Burlingame, CA 94010-4232
Tel: (650) 347-5010
Fax: (650) 347-5011
www.HLHibbardAttorney.com

Contents

Introduction 1

Chart .... 2 - 3

Chart Detailed Explanation of Real Property Categories

1. Single Family Dwelling, Purchase Money First 4

2. Single Family Dwelling, Purchase Money First, and Second Loans 6

3. Single Family Dwelling, Line of Credit Second 8

4. Single Family Dwelling, Refinanced Loans 10

5. Single Family Dwelling, 2nd Home 12

6. Residential Property, 4 Units or Less, Owner Occupied 14

7. Commercial Residential 16

8. Commercial Business 17

Further Reading

9. Walk Away From Your Home With Cash in Your Pocket and No Tax or Deficiency Liability 18

10. Mortgage Forgiveness Debt Relief Act of 2007 and California Conformity Act of 2010 Expire on December 21, 2012 20

11. Senate Bill 94 Advance Fees for Loan Modifications Now Prohibited 21

12. Senate Bill 931 and 458 Forgive All Debt After a Short Sale 22

13. Gave My House Keys to the Bank — Now I'm Being Sued! 23

14. Foreclosure Scams to Collect on Purchase Money 2nd or 3rd Deeds of Trust 25

15. Distressed Property Owners Who Receive a 1099-A, 1099-C May Face Serious Tax Consequences 27

16. Chapter 13 Bankruptcy Debtors: Eliminate 2nd and 3rd Mortgages by Lien Stripping! 29

17. Home Loss By Foreclosure During Loan Modifications — What Can Be Done About It? 30

About the Author 31

Notes 32

Disclaimer

1) The Distressed Property Owners' Options Chart gives general guidelines for distressed property owners. Owners should consult legal counsel prior to taking any course of action based on any option listed in the Chart.

2) This Chart does not apply to loans where any type of fraud occurred in obtaining the loan such as giving "stated income" which was not accurate to owner's actual income.

3) This Chart is dated as of November 23, 2011 and the legal basis for the Chart options may change without modification to the Chart. Legal counsel should be consulted prior to taking action on any choice outlined in the Chart to determine change of law or inapplicability for any reason.

4) This Chart was designed to apply to real estate owned and financed within the state of California.

5) This Chart applies only to property in which the lender uses non-judicial foreclosure.

For judicial foreclosure you must consult legal counsel.

Introduction

This booklet is designed to give distressed real property owners, along with real estate brokers, agents, and bankers, an overview of the various financial and legal options available to minimize negative financial impact.

The Distressed Property Owners' Options Chart and adjoining chapters reveal in a straight forward manner what every property owner needs to know to assess their situation and make an informed decision as to how to deal with their distressed property.

While real estate brokers, agents and bankers are not formally licensed to advise their distressed property owner clients, they still have a duty to insure their clients are informed of all their options. This booklet increases professional knowledge and thereby their ability to act as strong client advocates.

No specific choice should be acted upon by a property owner without consulting legal counsel and/or an accountant as each choice has specific requirements which are too numerous for the subject of this short treatise.

DISTRESSED PROPERTY

Type of Property* *Explanation for each type of property is listed in booklet	Loan Modification	Short Sale
1. Single Family Dwelling, Owner Occupied, Purchase Money First Loan	Yes	Yes
2. Single Family Dwelling, Purchase Money First and Second Loan	Yes	Yes
3. Single Family Dwelling, Purchase Money First and Second Loan (Line of Credit) Obtained at Purchase of Home	Yes	Yes
4. Single Family Dwelling, First and/or Second Loans Refinanced	Yes	Yes
5. Single Family Dwelling, Not Primary Residence, 2nd Home or Vacation	Yes, some banks which do not require owner occupied	Yes, some banks which do not require owner occupied
6. Residential property 4 Units or Less, Owner Occupied, Purchase Money Loans	Yes if Owner Occupied, Yes, some banks which do not require owner occupied	Yes, some banks which do not require owner occupied
7. Commercial Residential	No	No
8. Commercial Business	No	No

DISCLAIMERS: IMPORTANT - Chart subject to disclaimers; read disclaimer section.

OWNERS' OPTIONS CHART

Foreclosure Relief	Live Off Equity	Deficiency Liability	1099 A or C Liability	Deed in Lieu Option
Yes	Yes, until December 30, 2012 Mortgage Relief Act expires	None, until December 30, 2012 Mortgage Relief Act expires	None, until December 30, 2012 Mortgage Relief Act expires	Yes
Yes	Yes, until December 30, 2012 Mortgage Relief Act expires	Yes, until December 30, 2012 Mortgage Relief Act expires	No, until December 30, 2012 Mortgage Relief Act expires	Yes
Yes	Yes, but use Deed in Lieu before Foreclosure	Yes, if First Loan Forecloses	Yes, for Second Loan Amount	Yes
Yes	Yes, but use Deed in Lieu before Foreclosure	Yes, for Second Loan if First Loan uses Non-Judicial Foreclosure	Yes	Yes
Yes, some banks which do not require owner occupied	Not Applicable	Yes	Yes	Yes
Yes, some banks which do not require owner occupied	Yes, if Owner Occupied	No, if Owner Occupied	No, if Owner Occupied	Yes
No	Not Applicable	Yes	Yes	Yes
No	Not Applicable	Yes	Yes	Yes

www.HLHibbardAttorney.com

DISCLAIMERS: IMPORTANT - Chart subject to disclaimers; read disclaimer section.

1. Single Family Dwelling, Owner Occupied, Purchase Money First

If the above description fits your property, follow the Chart to the right of the property description.

Loan Modification: Yes: For information on modifying your loan consult http://www.makinghomeaffordable.gov/pages/default.aspx.

Short Sale: Yes: For information on obtaining lender approval for a short sale consult http://www.makinghomeaffordable.gov/pages/default.aspx.

Foreclosure Relief: Yes: For information on foreclosure benefits consult http://www.makinghomeaffordable.gov/pages/default.aspx.

Live Off Equity: Under the current law, an owner occupied home with a purchase money First Deed of Trust carries no income tax or deficiency liability. Therefore a property owner may elect to live in the property until the bank forecloses and not make any payments. In some cases, owners have remained in their homes for over a year. The reasonable rental value of the home is the equity and money the homeowner saves by not paying the mortgage or rent. One must either do a short sale or deed in lieu before December 30, 2012 when Federal and State Mortgage Relief Acts expire.

Deficiency Liability: No: Under the current law, an owner occupied home with a purchase money First Deed of Trust carries no deficiency liability under Code of Civil Procedure section 580(b). The lender is limited to foreclosing on the property. One must do either a short sale or deed in lieu before December 30, 2012 when Federal and State Mortgage Relief Acts expire.

1099 A or C Liability: No: If after foreclosure the homeowner receives a 1099 A or C, the homeowner should go to an accountant to file the proper IRS exemption form establishing the property was owner occupied at the time of foreclosure. One must either do a short sale or deed in lieu before December 30, 2012 when Federal and State Mortgage Relief Acts expire.

1. Single Family Dwelling, Owner Occupied, Purchase Money First

(continued)

Deed in Lieu: Yes: A property owner may always deed the property back to the bank. Homeowners who need to vacate the property for some reason and not live off their equity should deed the property back to the bank holding the First loan thereby avoid liability to governmental entities. For example: 1) Deficiency for First Loan; 2) Failure to maintain the property; 3) Liability for anyone who comes on the property and is injured; and 4) Kids who throw a party and someone is injured. The homeowners insurance should be kept in effect until the deed is recorded.

2. Single Family Dwelling, Owner Occupied, Purchase Money First, and Second Loans

If the above description fits your property, follow the Chart to the right of the property description.

Loan Modification: Yes: For information on modifying your loan consult http://www.makinghomeaffordable.gov/pages/default.aspx.

Short Sale: Yes: For information on obtaining lender approval for a short sale consult http://www.makinghomeaffordable.gov/pages/default.aspx.

Foreclosure Relief: Yes: For information on foreclosure benefits consult http://www.makinghomeaffordable.gov/pages/default.aspx.

Live Off Equity: Under the current law, an owner occupied home with a purchase money First and Second Deeds of Trust carries no income tax or deficiency liability. Therefore a property owner may elect to live in the property until the bank forecloses and not make any payments. In some cases, owners have remained in their homes for over a year. The reasonable rental value of the home is the equity and money the homeowner saves by not paying the mortgage or rent. One must either do a short sale or deed in lieu before December 30, 2012 when Federal and State Mortgage Relief Acts expire.

Deficiency Liability: No: Under the current law, an owner occupied home with a purchase money First and Second Deeds of Trust carries no deficiency liability under Code of Civil Procedure section 580(b). The lender is limited to foreclosing on the property. One must either do a short sale or deed in lieu before December 30, 2012 when Federal and State Mortgage Relief Acts expire.

1099 A or C Liability: No: If after foreclosure the homeowner receives a 1099 A or C, the homeowner should go to an accountant to file the proper IRS exemption form establishing the property was owner occupied at the time of foreclosure. One must either do a short sale or deed in lieu before December 30, 2012 when Federal and State Mortgage Relief Acts expire.

2. Single Family Dwelling, Owner Occupied, Purchase Money First, and Second Loans

(continued)

Deed in Lieu: Yes: A property owner may always deed the property back to the bank. Homeowners who need to vacate the property for some reason and not live off their equity should deed the property back to the bank holding the Second loan thereby avoid liability to governmental entities. For example: 1) Deficiency for unsecured Second Loan; 2) Failure to maintain the property; 3) Liability for anyone who comes on the property and is injured; and 4) Kids who throw a party and someone is injured. The homeowner's insurance should be kept in effect until the deed is recorded.

3. Single Family Dwelling, Owner Occupied, Purchase Money First and Second Loan (Line of Credit) Obtained at Purchase of Home

If the above description fits your property, follow the Chart to the right of the property description.

Loan Modification: Yes: For information on modifying your loan consult http://www.makinghomeaffordable.gov/pages/default.aspx.

Short Sale: Yes: For information on obtaining lender approval for a short sale consult http://www.makinghomeaffordable.gov/pages/default.aspx.

Foreclosure Relief: Yes: For information on foreclosure benefits consult http://www.makinghomeaffordable.gov/pages/default.aspx.

Live Off Equity: Yes: Under the current law, an owner occupied home with a purchase money First and Second Deeds of Trust carries no income tax or deficiency liability. Therefore a property owner may elect to live in the property until the bank forecloses and not make any payments. In some cases, owners have remained in their homes for over a year. The reasonable rental value of the home is the equity and money the homeowner saves by not paying the mortgage or rent.

However, a line of credit may not be considered a purchase money Second as it is a line of credit loan and not a normal purchase money loan. The law is not settled in this area, so to be safe consider a line of credit as if it is not protected by the anti-deficiency statute and not safe to live off equity until foreclosure. Prior to the bank's foreclosure sale, a deed in lieu should be recorded to the Second loan.

Deficiency Liability: Maybe: Under the current law, an owner occupied home with a purchase money First and Second Deeds of Trust carries no deficiency liability under Code of Civil Procedure section 580(b). The lender is limited to foreclosing on the property if he uses non-judicial foreclosure.

3. Single Family Dwelling, Owner Occupied, Purchase Money First and Second Loan (Line of Credit) Obtained at Purchase of Home

(continued)

However, if a line of credit loan is not considered "purchase money," a short sale or deed in lieu are the safest actions to take to avoid deficiency liability.

1099 A or C Liability: Maybe: If after foreclosure the homeowner receives a 1099 A or C, the homeowner should go to an accountant to file the proper IRS exemption form establishing the property was owner occupied at the time of foreclosure. If a line of credit loan is not considered a purchase loan, a short sale or deed in lieu are the safest actions to take to avoid deficiency liability under a 1099.

Deed in Lieu: Yes: A property owner may always deed the property back to the bank. Homeowners who need to vacate the property for some reason and not live off their equity should deed the property back to the bank holding the Second loan thereby avoid liability to governmental entities. For example: 1) Deficiency for unsecured Second Loan; 2) Failure to maintain the property; 3) Liability for anyone who comes on the property and is injured; and 4) Kids who throw a party and someone is injured. The homeowner's insurance should be kept in effect until the deed is recorded.

4. Single Family Dwelling, Owner Occupied, Refinanced First and/or Second Loan

If the above description fits your property, follow the Chart to the right of the property description.

Loan Modification: Yes: For information on modifying your loan consult http://www.makinghomeaffordable.gov/pages/default.aspx.

Short Sale: Yes: For information on obtaining lender approval for a short sale consult http://www.makinghomeaffordable.gov/pages/default.aspx.

Foreclosure Relief: Yes: For information on foreclosure benefits consult http://www.makinghomeaffordable.gov/pages/default.aspx.

Live Off Equity: Yes, however, the property should be sold in a short sale with permission from the Second mortgage lender or a Deed In Lieu recorded to the Second mortgage prior to the First mortgage foreclosing on the property. Both the short sale and Deed In Lieu avoid any deficiency or tax liability.

There is no deficiency if the foreclosure is non-judicial as under "One Action," California Code of Civil Procedure section 580(b), the lender is limited to the property. Therefore if the First loan forecloses non-judicially, the Second becomes an unsecured obligation of the borrower, but there is no deficiency on the foreclosing First loan. In some cases, owners have remained in their homes for over a year. The reasonable rental value of the home is the equity and money the homeowner saves by not paying the mortgage or rent.

Deficiency Liability: Yes: Under the current law, an owner occupied home with a refinanced First and/or Second Deeds of Trust carries deficiency liability for the amount of the Second loan if the First loan forecloses non-judicially.

Under Code of Civil Procedure section 580(b), the foreclosing lender is limited to the property. There is deficiency liability for any judicial forclosure although this is very rare for single family dwellings.

4. Single Family Dwelling, Owner Occupied, Refinanced First and/or Second Loan

(continued)

1099 A or C Liability: Yes: If after foreclosure the homeowner receives a 1099 A or C, the homeowner should go to an accountant to file the proper IRS exemption form establishing the property was owner occupied at the time of foreclosure. A short sale or deed in lieu are the safest actions to take to avoid deficiency liability under a 1099.

Deed in Lieu: Yes: A property owner may always deed the property back to the bank. Homeowners who need to vacate the property for some reason and not live off their equity should deed the property back to the bank holding the Second loan thereby avoid liability to governmental entities. For example: 1) Deficiency for unsecured Second Loan; 2) Failure to maintain the property; 3) Liability for anyone who comes on the property and is injured; and 4) Kids who throw a party and someone is injured. The homeowner's insurance should be kept in effect until the deed is recorded.

5. Single Family Dwelling, 2nd Home or Vacation Home

If the above description fits your property, follow the Chart to the right of the property description.

Loan Modification: Yes: For information on modifying your loan consult http://www.makinghomeaffordable.gov/pages/default.aspx.

Short Sale: Yes: For information on obtaining lender approval for a short sale consult http://www.makinghomeaffordable.gov/pages/default.aspx.

Foreclosure Relief: Yes: For information on foreclosure benefits consult http://www.makinghomeaffordable.gov/pages/default.aspx.

Live Off Equity: No: Under the current law, a Second or Vacation home carries possible income tax and deficiency liability. A property owner should short sale and/or deed in lieu to the Second loan, or if only one loan, deed to the First Loan before the foreclosure sale is complete to avoid deficiency.

There is no deficiency if the foreclosure is non-judicial as under "One Action," California Code of Civil Procedure section 580(b), the lender is limited to the property. Therefore if the First loan forecloses non-judicially, the Second becomes an unsecured obligation of the borrower, but there is no deficiency on the foreclosing First loan.

Deficiency Liability: Yes: Under the current law, a Second Home or Vacation home with First and/or Second Deeds of Trust carries deficiency liability for the amount of the Second loan if the First loan forecloses non-judicially. Under Code of Civil Procedure section 580(b), the foreclosing lender is limited to the property. There is deficiency liability for any judicial foreclosure although this is very rare for single family dwellings.

1099 A or C Liability: Yes: If after foreclosure the homeowner receives a 1099 A or C, the homeowner should go to an accountant for tax advice.

5. Single Family Dwelling, 2nd Home or Vacation Home

(continued)

A short sale or deed in lieu are the safest actions to take to avoid deficiency liability under a 1099.

Deed in Lieu: Yes: A property owner may always deed the property back to the bank. Homeowners who have vacated the property for some reason should deed the property back to the bank holding the Second loan, or if only one loan to the First, thereby avoid liability to governmental entities. For example: 1) Deficiency for unsecured Second Loan; 2) Failure to maintain the property; 3) Liability for anyone who comes on the property and is injured; and 4) Kids who throw a party and someone is injured. The homeowners insurance should be kept in effect until the deed is recorded.

6. Residential Property, 4 Units or Less, Owner Occupied, Purchase Money Loans

If the above description fits your property, follow the Chart to the right of the property description.

Loan Modification: Yes: For information on modifying your loan consult http://www.makinghomeaffordable.gov/pages/default.aspx.

Short Sale: Yes: For information on obtaining lender approval for a short sale consult http://www.makinghomeaffordable.gov/pages/default.aspx.

Foreclosure Relief: Yes: For information on foreclosure benefits consult http://www.makinghomeaffordable.gov/pages/default.aspx.

Live Off Equity: Under the current law, an owner occupied home with a purchase money First and Second Deeds of Trust carries no income tax or deficiency liability. Therefore a property owner may elect to live in the property until the bank forecloses and not make any payments. In some cases, owners have remained in their homes for over a year. The reasonable rental value of the home is the equity and money the homeowner saves by not paying the mortgage or rent. One must either do a short sale or deed in lieu before December 30, 2012 when Federal and State Mortgage Relief Acts expire.

Deficiency Liability: No: Under the current law, an owner occupied home with a purchase money First and Second Deeds of Trust carries no deficiency liability under Code of Civil Procedure section 580(b). The lender is limited to foreclosing on the property. One must either do a short sale or deed in lieu before December 30, 2012 when Federal and State Mortgage Relief Acts expire.

1099 A or C Liability: No: If after foreclosure the homeowner receives a 1099 A or C, the homeowner should go to an accountant to file the proper IRS exemption form establishing the property was owner occupied at the time of foreclosure. One must either do a short sale or deed in lieu before December 30, 2012 when Federal and State Mortgage Relief Acts expire.

6. Residential Property, 4 Units or Less, Owner Occupied, Purchase Money Loans

(continued)

Deed in Lieu: Yes: A property owner may always deed the property back to the bank. Homeowners who need to vacate the property for some reason and not live off their equity should deed the property back to the bank holding the Second loan thereby avoid liability to governmental entities. For example: 1) Deficiency for unsecured Second Loan; 2) Failure to maintain the property; 3) Liability for anyone who comes on the property and is injured; and 4) Kids who throw a party and someone is injured. The homeowner's insurance should be kept in effect until the deed is recorded.

7. Commercial Residential Property

If the above description fits your property, follow the Chart to the right of the property description.

Loan Modification: No

Short Sale: No

Foreclosure Relief: No

Live Off Equity: Not Applicable

Deficiency Liability: Yes

1099 A or C Liability: Yes

Deed in Lieu: Yes

8. Commercial Business Property

If the above description fits your property, follow the Chart to the right of the property description.

Loan Modification: No

Short Sale: No

Foreclosure Relief: No

Live Off Equity: Not Applicable

Deficiency Liability: Yes

1099 A or C Liability: Yes

Deed in Lieu: Yes

9. Walk Away From Your Home with Cash in Your Pocket and No Tax or Deficiency Liability

CONCEPT:

In the State of California, a homeowner may execute a deed in lieu of foreclosure to the bank whose loan is secured by a deed of trust. A deed of trust is the same as a mortgage in other states. The deed of trust is recorded in the county where the home is located. A deed in lieu allows a homeowner to transfer ownership of their home to the bank that owns the loan. The loan is canceled by operation of law, as a secured owner of a loan cannot be the owner of the property and hold a secured interest against the property at the same time.

The deed in lieu should deed the property to the most recent bank loan on record. For example, if there are first and second mortgages, then both loans are secured by deeds of trust. The deed in lieu should deed the property to the holder of the second loan. If there are three mortgages, then the deed in lieu should deed the home to the third and so on. A deed in lieu protects the homeowner from being responsible for all types of loans whether purchase money or refinanced. (See Mortgages, Deeds of Trust and Foreclosure Litigation, Continuing Education of the Bar, Oakland, CA, available at your local law library).

PROCEDURE:

After the deed in lieu is recorded, it must be mailed to the bank by Certified Mail Return Receipt Requested as well as regular mail. The bank has a reasonable time to reject the deed in lieu, say 6 months. In my 30 years experience handling hundreds of deeds in lieu, I have never had a bank reject one.

Unless the bank receiving the deed in lieu rejects it [as required by California Civil Code section 1058.5(a)], then the transfer is deemed a full credit sale. A full credit sale protects the homeowner from 1099 taxes and any deficiency.

9. Walk Away From Your Home with Cash in Your Pocket and No Tax or Deficiency Liability

(continued)

A deed in lieu is just as if a sale of the property occurred and the sale price was equal to the amount of all the loans secured by all the deeds of trust.

REQUESTING MONEY TO VACATE THE HOME:

When one of the bank lenders contacts the homeowner regarding obtaining possession of their home, either before foreclosure, after foreclosure, or when the homeowner receives a Three-Day Notice to Vacate, the homeowner is to prepare a document in writing per the directions on the website: www.MakingHomeAffordable.gov. After you open the site, click on: "Explore Programs." When that choice opens, click on: "Leave Your Home and Avoid Foreclosure," and after that web page opens, click on: "Exit Gracefully." This website explains how the homeowner may receive $3,000 to $5,000 to voluntarily vacate the home.

CONCLUSION:

A deed in lieu is a valuable tool to protect the homeowner from any deficiency or tax liability. It puts money in their pocket for a home that's valued at less than the secured loans and proved to be a bad investment. The deed in lieu protects the homeowner if the owner has experienced changed conditions of income that prevent paying the loans.

The Law Office of Howard L. Hibbard is available to prepare a deed in lieu and all transfer documents. The fixed fee includes guidance on recording the deed to meet County Recorder requirements and providing up to three letters to any bank attorney.

10. Mortgage Forgiveness Debt Relief Act of 2007 and California Conformity Act of 2010 Expire on December 21, 2012

The owner who occupies his home and loses his property by foreclosure historically faced either a lawsuit for any deficiency on the loan or loans and/or a 1099 for the amount not covered by the proceeds of the foreclosure sale. The amount of the loan or loans not satisfied by the foreclosure sale proceeds is called Debt Relief. The amount of debt relieved is considered taxable ordinary income in the year the foreclosure occurred and the lender could issue a Form 1099 to the former owner of the property.

The Mortgage Debt Relief Act of 2007 generally allows taxpayers to exclude income from the discharge of debt relief income on their principle residence. This act is in full force and effect until December 31, 2012. A homeowner who loses his principle residence by foreclosure and receives a IRS Form 1099(a) or 1099(c) should file a IRS Form 982 with his tax return. This form will exempt the 1099 deficiency amount from his income. There are limitations on the amount of debt relief income which is forgiven which need to be discussed with an accountant.

In April 2010 the Conformity Act of 2010 was enacted by the State of California and is in full force and effect until December 31, 2012. This act adopts the provisions of the IRS Mortgage Forgiveness Debt Relief Act of 2007 and allows taxpayers who had all or part of the loan balance on their principle residence forgiven after foreclosure. This act also has limitations on the amount of debt relief income that may be forgiven.

Homeowners who are in the process of a short sale or loan modification in November and December 2012 should consider a deed in lieu of foreclosure if it appears the loan modification or short sale process is not going to close by December 31, 2012. If the loan modification or short sale fails to close and the homeowner loses the property by foreclosure the homeowner faces debt relief income as well as possible loan deficiency liability.

11. Senate Bill 94 Advance Fees for Loan Modifications Now Prohibited

In 2009, the State of California adopted Senate Bill 94. This bill prohibits the collection of advance fees when obtaining a loan modification. Violation of this act is subject to a fine of not more than $10,000.00, imprisonment for up to a year and/or both.

There are exceptions for licensed real estate professionals and attorneys, but generally a homeowner should only pay loan modification fees at the close of escrow.

12. Senate Bill 931 and 458 Forgive All Debt After a Short Sale

Senate Bill 931, enacted CCP §580e, which became effective in January of 2011, provides that when a residential lender in the first deed of trust approves in writing a short sale of 1-4 unit properties, the lender cannot later seek payment for the unpaid loan balance.

CCP 580e, reads in part, *"... Written consent of the holder of the first deed of trust or first mortgage to that sale shall obligate that holder to accept the sale proceeds as full payment and to fully discharge the remaining amount of the indebtedness on the first deed of trust or first mortgage."*

For example, if the lender who has a first loan for $500,000 agrees to a short sale for $400,000, the lender is prohibited from going after the homeowner for the $100,000 that is not covered by the short sale purchase at $400,000.

Senate Bill 458 was enacted in July of 2011 to expand ant-deficiency protection to first, second and subsequent mortgages in a short sale of 1-4 unit properties. Senate Bill 931 only applied to first mortgages and only prohibited the first lien holders from pursuing a deficiency judgment following a short sale. Senate Bill 458 closes the loop left by Senate Bill 931, which only applied to first mortgages.

For example, a house has a first loan of $500,000 and a second loan of $100,000 for a total loan of $600,000. If both lenders agree to a short sale of $400,000 with the first lender to receive $350,000 and the second lender to receive $50,000, neither lender may go after the homeowner for the $200,000 not covered by the short sale.

13. Gave My House Keys to the Bank – Now I'm Being Sued!

You are unable to make your mortgage payments. You received a foreclosure notice from the bank so you surrendered your keys, moved out, and canceled your homeowner's insurance. You think you are off the hook. So, how can you be sued for problems on your vacant property?

The problem is that while the bank gave notice of pending foreclosure, the homeowner is still liable for any problems on their property until the title transfers to the bank. Complaints that others make to the City, County or Homeowners' Association against your property, i.e. not being maintained; nuisances like kids throwing parties; or homeowner fees still due, are examples of the homeowner's continued personal responsibility.

If you are still on title, you are still personally liable for all criminal liability for failure to maintain the property; civil liability for any person injured on your property; still owe homeowner fees; and more.

The solution is simple. Until you are off title, you are still liable. As long as you are on title, you need to keep paying your homeowner's insurance premiums.

The best way to solve the problem if the bank does not complete the foreclosure on your home is to record a DEED IN LIEU OF FORECLOSURE. However, in some states, the bank must approve the Deed In Lieu. California is not one of those states, but there are issues to be considered which are too are lengthy for this brief description for which you should obtain legal counsel.

A Deed In Lieu of Foreclosure is a deed from the owner to the first or second deed of trust or mortgage holder. The property owner is to acquire the form Quitclaim Deed and type or write beside this title, "In Lieu of Foreclosure" so the whole title reads,"Quitclaim Deed In Lieu of Foreclosure."

13. Gave My House Keys to the Bank — Now I'm Being Sued!

(continued)

To obtain more information about Deeds in Lieu, read the book: MORTGAGES, DEEDS OF TRUST AND FORECLOSURE LITIGATION, CONTINUING EDUCATION OF THE BAR, CALIFORNIA OAKLAND, CALIFORNIA, January 2010, Chapter Title, Debtor's Strategies, section 7.11, page 523; 7.127.21, page 524 and 7.21A, page 530.

To find more information on the web try doing a search using the phrase, "Deed In Lieu."

14. Foreclosure Scams to Collect on Purchase Money 2nd or 3rd Deeds of Trust

Senate Bill 931 which enacts California Code of Civil Procedure §580e became effective January 1, 2011.

C.C.P. §580e prohibits recovery of a deficiency on a first deed of trust following a short sale of real property of four (4) units or less because C.C.P. §580e(a), read, in part: "....Written consent of the holder of the first deed of trust or first mortgage to that sale shall obligate that holder to accept the sale proceeds as FULL PAYMENT and to fully discharge the remaining amount of the indebtedness on the first deed of trust or first mortgage."

This means you should not get a 1099-A or 1099-C from the holder of the first deed of trust following a short sale! For more information on 1099-A or 1099-C, please read Chapter 15.

What C.C.P. §580(e) does not address are second deeds of trust or other non-purchase money loans on real property. Lenders with second or third deeds of trust and/or lines of credit may still, and have been, suing short sale borrowers to recover monies borrowed.

The question then becomes, what is the state of the law for when both the first and second deed of trust were used to purchase the property? Interestingly in 2009, the Northern District of California ruled that a second deed of trust, made concurrently with a first deed of trust for the purchase of real property is a purchase money loan within the meaning of C.C.P. §580(b). See Herrera v. LCS Fin. Servs. Corp. (ND Cal. 2009)

BEWARE OF SCAMS TO COLLECT
ON PURCHASE MONEY 2nd or 3rd DEEDS OF TRUST

The Herrera case holds that purchase money 2nd or 3rd deeds of trust are subject to anti-deficiency law as outlined in C.C.P. 580c. Some lenders are attempting to collect on junior purchase money deeds of trust after

14. Foreclosure Scams to Collect on Purchase Money 2nd or 3rd Deeds of Trust

(continued)

foreclosure or demand a deficiency in a short sale.

The lender is not entitled to demand a deficiency after foreclosure on a purchase money 2nd or 3rd deed of trust.

Any attempt to collect on an uncollectable debt, without the collection agency stating re-payment is not mandatory, may be grounds to sue the collection agency for violation of California Fair Debt Collections Act.

STRATEGY TO REQUEST MINIMUM OR NO DEFICIENCY ON A PURCHASE MONEY 2ND OR 3RD DEED OF TRUST UNDER A SHORT SALE

As a realtor, if you are negotiating the short sale with a junior purchase money deed of trust, you must make it clear to the lender that through the short sale, the lender is actually saving: 1) Months of non-payment on the loan; 2) Months of vacancy; 3) Costs of foreclosure proceedings; and 4) Costs of resale. In addition, there is no right to a deficiency after a foreclosure. Disclosure of these realities should create a stronger bargaining position to facilitate a short sale for a minimum or no deficiency.

15. Distressed Property Owners Who Receive a 1099-A, 1099-C May Face Serious Tax Consequences

Serious tax consequences may result from either a short sale or foreclosure. As with most IRS information, it is not an exciting read, but you could save yourself thousands of dollars in taxes.

Many distressed property owners who have left their home or lost their property by foreclosure will receive a 1099-A, 1099-C or both from the lenders. Lenders are required to file the 1099's with the IRS and mail a copy to the borrower. Depending on the form you receive, you could be liable for thousands of dollars in additional taxes.

What do these tax forms mean? By definition, a 1099-A is for "Acquisition or Abandonment of Real Property" and a 1099-C is for "Cancellation of Debt." This article outlines the circumstances in which you may receive a 1099-A and/ or 1099-C. If you do receive a 1099-A or 1099-C, it is important to contact your accountant or tax preparer immediately to discuss the tax consequences and any possible exemptions under updated IRS Form 982.

1099-A: The lender's responsibility to file the 1099-A is triggered when the lender acquires an interest in the property that is the security for the loan. It does not matter if the interest acquired represents a full or partial satisfaction of the debt.

A 1099-A must be filed in three (3) situations:

1. Foreclosure: Regardless of whether the lender is the first, second or third mortgage holder, upon foreclosure of the property, all lenders are required to file a 1099-A for the amount of the debt. The 1099-A is required if there is a deficiency and the lender does attempt to collect the deficiency from the borrower. The lender is required to file if they know or have reason to know the foreclosure has taken place.

2. Abandonment: If the borrower intends to, and has permanently given up

15. Distressed Property Owners Who Receive a 1099-A or 1099-C May Face Serious Tax Consequences

(continued)

possession and use of the property, the lender must file a 1099-A. If a foreclosure will be performed within three (3) months of the abandonment by the borrower, the lender may wait to file the 1099-A until the date of the foreclosure sale. If a foreclosure is not scheduled within three (3) months of the abandonment, the lender must file the 1099-A within three (3) months of the date of abandonment.

3. Claim and Delivery: Claim and delivery is a legal action to recover property, for 1099-A purposes, only property that is security for a debt. A 1099-A is required if the property is used for business, trade or investment purposes. Property solely for personal use does not trigger the requirement to file a 1099-A.

1099-C: The lender's responsibility to file a 1099-C is triggered when the lender acquires an interest in the property that is the security for a loan and the lender forgives, cancels or discharges the debt. Canceled debt must be reported as "gross income" and the borrower will be required to pay tax thereon unless the debt qualifies for an exclusion or exception.

1. Debt cancellation: Lenders who cancel, forgive or discharge any debt for $600.00 or more are required to file a 1099-C with the IRS.

2. Foreclosure: Regardless of whether the lender is the first, second or third mortgage holder, upon foreclosure of the property, all lenders are required to file a 1099-A. The 1099-C is required if there is a deficiency and the lender does not attempt to collect the deficiency from the borrower. If the debt is canceled, the lender need only file a 1099-C and not a 1099-A.

When a borrower receives a 1099-A or 1099-C, the IRS has already received the form. You must address the tax issues immediately by filing an updated IRS Form 982. Failure to do so may result in penalties and fees.

16. Chapter 13 Bankruptcy Debtors: Eliminate 2nd and 3rd Mortgages by Lien Stripping!

Chapter 13 Bankruptcy debtors have the amazing opportunity to save hundreds of thousands of dollars. See Zimmer v. PSB Lending Corporation (In RE: Zimmer) 313 F3d 1220 (9th Cir. 2002). Debtors can strip the Second and Third Mortgages ("Junior Mortgages") on their home with a relatively straightforward motion to the Court. Stripping the Junior Mortgages means that for the purpose of the Debtors' Chapter 13 bankruptcy plan, the Junior Mortgages are valued at zero (0) and no payments will be made!!

After completing the Plan payments, Debtors can obtain a judgment voiding the Junior Mortgages. This means that the Debtors will have absolutely no further obligation to pay the Junior Mortgages... ever!!

Generally, a mortgage is a secured debt because it is attached to real property, however, if the value of the property has declined to the point where the value is less that the amount owing on the First Mortgage, the Junior Mortgages become unsecured.

In order to strip a Second Mortgage, several simple conditions must be met: 1) The property must be the Debtors' primary residence; and 2) The current value of the Property must be less than the amount due on the First Mortgage.

If both of these conditions are met, the Debtor can make a motion to have their Junior Mortgages stripped! You may visit the Bankruptcy Court website in your area for more information and guidelines.

The Law Office of Howard L. Hibbard specializes in preparing Lien Strip Motions. A significant portion of our business in this area comes from bankruptcy attorney referrals.

17. Home Loss By Foreclosure During Loan Modifications – What Can Be Done About It?

Home loss by foreclosure during loan modifications has been on the rise. Senators Mark Leno (D-San Francisco), and Darrell Steinberg (D-Sacramento), recently proposed new legislation that would forbid lenders from starting foreclosure proceedings against homeowners who have a loan modification request pending. Their Senate Bill 729, would have provided checks and balances for responsible lending, including but not limited to: 1) A "Yes" or "No" from the lender to the homeowner on the loan modification before the lender begins foreclosure proceedings; 2) Proof of ownership of the note by the lender at the time the lender records the default; 3) Lifetime loan accounting from the servicer to the homeowner at the time of the notice of default; and 4) Limited legal resources to the buyer.

To protect yourself and your home, the Law Office of Howard L. Hibbard strongly recommends that the homeowner and/or modification facilitator obtain the name and contact information of the person handing both the modification and the foreclosure and provide the same to all involved parties. Further, all communications from the homeowner and/or modification facilitator should be sent to both the loan modification and foreclosure department contacts by Certified Mail Return Receipt Requested. You need to create a paper trail to protect yourself.

Utilize the www.makinghomeaffordable.gov website for Home Affordable Modification Program (HAMP) forms and information. Also read helpful pamphlets, obtain contact information for lenders and watch informational videos. Home Affordable Foreclosure Alternatives (HAFA) information is also available.

About the Author

Howard L. Hibbard is owner and principal attorney of the Law Office of Howard L. Hibbard, founded in 1979. With over 30 years experience as a trial attorney in both state and federal courts, his primary focus has been on commercial and residential real estate matters, including construction defect lawsuits.

In addition, his clients rely upon him for business law, corporate and insurance litigation, debt collection, bankruptcy adversary actions, labor relations and elder law.

He has extensive experience in real estate and construction defect litigation, with a case history of achieving multi-million dollar settlements involving large housing developments, commercial properties and condominium complexes. He has served as chief legal counsel for a major soil engineering company since 1981, where he has handled lawsuits involving housing developments with as many as 250 homes in a single case.

Mr. Hibbard is also author of *The Legal Pitfalls of Short Sales and Foreclosures*, and teaches seminars on how to avoid foreclosure through loan modification programs, and other important information on buying and selling distressed properties.

Law Office of Howard L. Hibbard

Notes

Notes

www.ingramcontent.com/pod-product-compliance
Lightning Source LLC
Chambersburg PA
CBHW032256210326
41520CB00048B/4228

* 9 7 8 0 9 8 5 6 3 4 4 0 7 *